BOOM SCIENCE

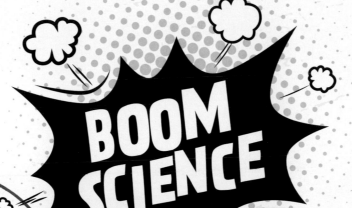

FORCES

Georgia Amson-Bradshaw

WAYLAND

www.waylandbooks.co.uk

First published in Great Britain in 2018 by Wayland

Copyright © Hodder and Stoughton Limited, 2018

 Produced for Wayland by
White-Thomson Publishing Ltd
www.wtpub.co.uk

Series Editor: Georgia Amson-Bradshaw
Series Designer: Rocket Design (East Anglia) Ltd

ISBN: 978 1 5263 0658 6
10 9 8 7 6 5 4 3 2 1

Wayland
An imprint of
Hachette Children's Group
Part of Hodder & Stoughton
Carmelite House
50 Victoria Embankment
London EC4Y 0DZ

An Hachette UK Company
www.hachette.co.uk
www.hachettechildrens.co.uk

Printed in China

Picture acknowledgements:
lady-luck 6t, Lucky Business 6b, chrupka 7b, fotum 7b, thka 7b, gpointstudio 7b, tynyuk 8, Andrew Rybalko 9b, Grigorita Ko 10t, adichrisworo 10b, Rimma Z 11t, Sergej Cash 11b, Helioscribe 12t, Sabelskaya 12b, Halfpoint 13t, Lorelyn Medina 13b, Pretty Vectors 16, Mascha Tace 17t, Scanrail1 17c, horiyan 17c, vectorsector 18t, zaferkizilkaya 18b, Parinya Panyana 19t, feathercollector 19c, Valentin Valkov 19b, Pat_Hastings 22t, Petar An 22b, MarinaMay 23t, pippeeContributor 24b, Mopic 25t, MuchMania 25c, Olga Popova 25b

All illustrations on pages 12, 13, 18, 19, 22, 23 by Steve Evans

All design elements from Shutterstock.

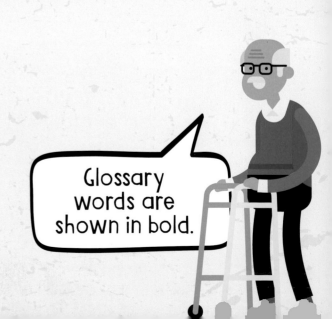

Glossary words are shown in bold.

CONTENTS

WHAT IS A FORCE?

A force is a push or a pull.

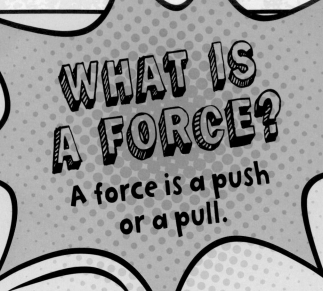

I am being forced to stand still!

AND... ACTION!

Forces make things happen. They make objects move, change shape, change direction, speed up or slow down. They even make things stay still.

PUSHES AND PULLS

You can't see a force, but you can see what it does. Forces push and pull things. If you hit a tennis ball with a racket, that is a pushing force. When the ball falls to the ground, it is because it is pulled by the force of **gravity**.

6

STRONG AND WEAK

Some forces are very strong. The Earth's gravity is a strong pulling force that keeps everything from floating off into space. Some forces are weak. If you blow gently on an object, that is a weak pushing force.

HEY, WHAT AM I?

What are the pushing or pulling forces being **applied** in these pictures? Answer on page 28.

FORCES IN ACTION

Forces can be balanced or unbalanced.

MANY FORCES

There is almost always more than one force acting on an object at the same time. For example, when we kick a ball into the air, we see the effect of the push. But the kick is not the only force acting on the ball.

Air resistance is pushing back on the ball.

Force is pushing the ball upwards.

Gravity is pulling downwards on the ball, even as it soars into the air.

The forces pushing and pulling on the ball are all acting with different strengths.

UNBALANCED FORCES

When one force is stronger than the others, the forces are unbalanced. Unbalanced forces make objects change speed, direction or shape, such as this skier who is getting faster as they go down the slope. The gravity pulling them downwards is stronger than the **friction** between the snow and their skis.

Don't just sit still, help me tidy the house!

BALANCED FORCES

When the forces are all equal, they cancel each other out. The object will stay completely still. If it is already moving, it will stay moving at the same speed and without changing direction.

I'm studying the effects of balanced forces.

GRAVITY

Objects are pulled towards each other by gravity.

THE EARTH'S PULL

When you drop something, it falls down. That's because it is pulled down by the Earth's gravity. Gravity is a **non-contact** force, which means the Earth and the object don't have to be touching for the effect to happen.

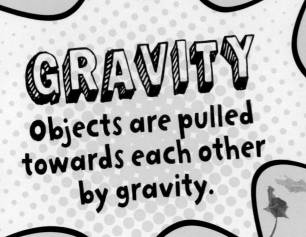

FORCES IN SPACE

The Earth's gravitational pull doesn't just make things fall to the ground. It keeps the Moon in **orbit**, too. Without gravity, the Moon would float off elsewhere in space.

We've always been close ...

FRICTION

When surfaces rub together, they create friction.

RUBBING TOGETHER

Unlike gravity, friction is a **contact force**. It is created when two surfaces are moving, or trying to move across each other. Friction stops or slows the movement down. Friction stops these cars from sliding down the hill.

ROUGH AND SMOOTH

More friction is created between rough surfaces than smooth surfaces. Think about sliding in your socks across a shiny floor. You can't slide across rough carpet in the same way, because there is more friction.

STOP IN ORDER TO GO

By stopping surfaces sliding, friction can actually help things move! Friction is what makes the wheels on a car or wheelchair **grip** the ground as they turn. This makes the car or wheelchair move forward instead of spinning on the spot.

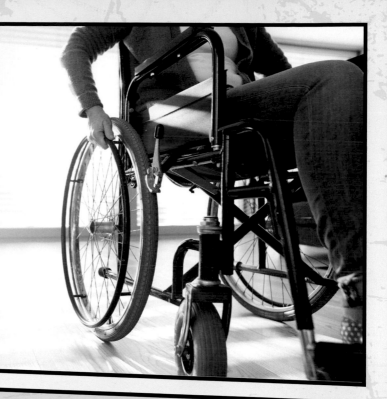

Friction produces heat. You can even start a fire using friction by spinning a wooden stick against a wooden board, until the heat starts a fire.

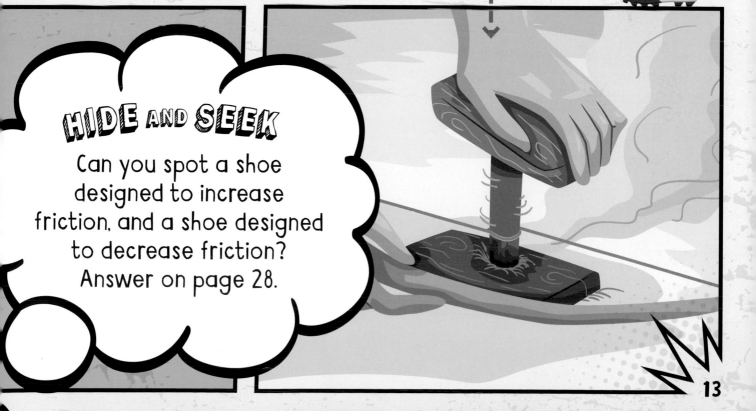

HIDE AND SEEK

Can you spot a shoe designed to increase friction, and a shoe designed to decrease friction? Answer on page 28.

YOUR TURN!

RICE FRICTION TRICK

Use friction to beat gravity with this cool experiment. You'll need:

rice

A bag of rice

A 500 ml plastic drinks bottle

A wooden chopstick

STEP ONE

Fill the bottle with dry rice, and poke the wooden chopstick right down into it.

STEP TWO

Pull upwards on the chopstick. What happens?

STEP THREE

Tap the bottle of rice firmly on a hard surface a number of times. The aim is to compact the rice and get rid of air pockets. You may need to top the bottle up with more rice.

STEP FOUR

Push the chopstick all the way into the rice again. Try lifting the chopstick. What happens this time? If the rice has been compacted enough, pulling on the chopstick should lift up the whole bottle. If it doesn't work, try tapping the bottle again, adding more rice or leaving it to settle for a while.

How does this trick work? Answer on page 29.

AIR RESISTANCE

Objects moving through air are slowed down by a force called air resistance.

SLOWING A FALL

How could someone jump out of a plane hundreds of metres up in the air, and land safely? By using something designed to increase air resistance – a parachute!

air resistance

Excuse me – coming through!

PUSH BACK

Although we often think of air as being empty space, it's actually a material. When you move through air, it pushes back against you. Big objects, such as a parachute, create a large surface for the air to push against.

Eeek!

SPEED AND RESISTANCE

The faster something is moving through the air, the more air resistance pushes back on it. That's why you can feel air rushing past your face when you whizz downhill on your scooter, but not when you walk around.

Can't catch us!

HEY, WHAT AM I?

Which vehicle will experience the most air resistance when moving? Answer on page 29.

WOW!

Because there is no air on the Moon, there is no air resistance. A parachute would be useless on the Moon!

WATER RESISTANCE

Objects moving through water are slowed down by water resistance.

PUSHING FORCE

Just like objects moving through air, objects moving through water have a force pushing back on them, called **water resistance**.

water resistance

STREAMLINING

It is possible to reduce the effect of air resistance or water resistance by making objects **streamlined**. This means making them into thin, pointy shapes. Most fish have slim, pointy bodies to help them move faster through water.

Slow down, I can't keep up!

USING RESISTANCE

Water resistance can be useful, too. If you want to move through water, you can push against the water to **propel** yourself forwards. This is how fish use their tail fins, and people rowing boats use **oars**.

Flying fish can glide along in the air above the ocean, while keeping their tail in the water to push themselves along using water resistance.

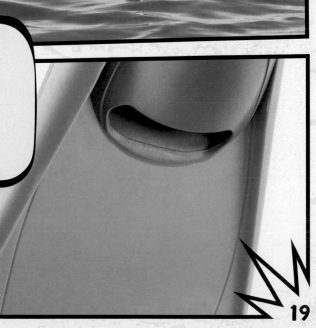

HEY, WHAT AM I?

The objects in this picture use water resistance to work. What are they? Answer on page 29.

YOUR TURN!

STREAMLINED SHAPES

Discover which shapes can reduce water resistance with this experiment. You'll need:

Scissors

Two 2-litre clear plastic drinks bottles

Modelling clay

Water

STEP ONE

Ask an adult to cut the tops off the two plastic bottles, and fill them up with water. Make sure the water level is the same in both bottles.

Take equal-sized pieces of modelling clay, and mould them into different shapes, such as a flat disc, a round ball and any other shape you'd like to test. It is important that each piece of modelling clay weighs the same amount to make it a fair test.

STEP THREE

Drop a piece of modelling clay into each bottle at exactly the same time and from the same height. Watch to see which of the two shapes reaches the bottom of the bottle first. Test all of your shapes against each other to find out which shape sinks through the water the fastest and which sinks the slowest. The piece that sinks the fastest is the most streamlined shape.

MAGNETIC FORCE

Magnetic force is a non-contact force created by magnets.

PUSH OR PULL

Magnets have a **magnetic force** which can pull certain materials and push or pull other magnets. Like gravity, it is a non-contact force which means a magnet does not have to touch the other object to push or pull it.

TYPES OF MAGNET

Magnets come in many shapes and sizes, from small horseshoe magnets to huge circular magnets used to lift scrap metal.

MAGNETIC METALS

Most materials, such as plastic or wood, are not magnetic. This means magnets can't push or pull them. Most types of metal are magnetic, and are pulled towards magnets.

What took you so long? Was it the dragon?

Um, no, my armour got stuck to the fridge door.

HIDE AND SEEK

Can you spot a bar magnet hiding? Answer on page 29.

USING MAGNETS

We use magnets for all sorts of things, such as keeping fridge doors closed and storing information on a computer's **hard drive**.

MAGNETIC POLES

Magnets have a north and a south pole.

TWO ENDS

The north pole of one magnet will **repel** the north pole of another magnet. It will **attract** the south pole of another magnet.

two unlike poles together attract

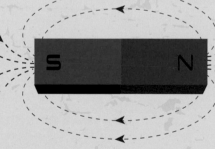

two like poles together repel

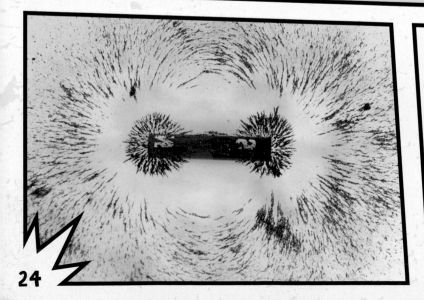

MAGNETIC FIELD

The area that a magnet affects is called its **magnetic field**. The magnetic force from the magnet is strongest at the two poles.

ENDS OF THE EARTH

In the centre of the Earth is a giant ball of iron, which turns the Earth into a huge, weak magnet. The Earth has a magnetic north and south pole, and a magnetic field.

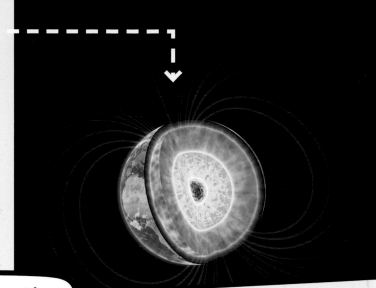

Hmm, the north pole was here yesterday...

WOW!

The exact location of the Earth's magnetic north pole changes a little bit each day, because some of the metal in the centre of the Earth is **liquid** and it moves around.

HEY, WHAT AM I?

This object uses the Earth's magnetic field. What is it? Answer on page 29.

40

20

0

NE

MAGNETIC MODEL KITE

Explore how big a magnet's magnetic field is with this experiment. You'll need:

A block of polystyrene

Coloured paper

A sharp pencil or skewer

A disc magnet

Scissors

Sticky tape

A large metal paper clip

Thread

STEP ONE

Cut a small kite shape out of the coloured paper, about four centimetres across. Draw a design on the front if you like, and tape the paper clip to the back of it. Tape the magnet to the blunt end of the pencil or skewer.

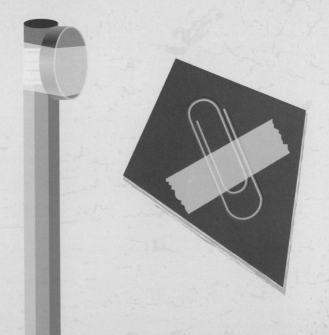

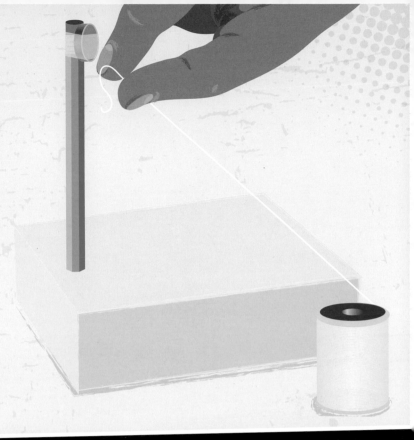

Poke the sharp end of the pencil down into the polystyrene block so that the pencil stands straight upwards with the magnet at the top. With the thread, check the distance from the magnet to the far edge of the polystyrene block.

Cut the thread a bit longer than that distance. Tape one end to the little paper kite. Holding the opposite end of the thread, see how far away from the magnet you can hold the kite and still have it hover in the air. Tape the other end of the tape to the edge of the block. Leave your little model kite floating in the air through magnetic force.

ANSWERS

Page 7   What am I?

1 A foot pushing down on a pedal.

2 The dog is pulling on the lead.

3 Someone pulling a hairbrush through hair.

Page 11

What am I? Trick question! Gravity is pulling down on everything in this picture, including the bungee jumping woman, the man, the bridge, the water – even the air in the sky!

Page 13

Hide and Seek An ice skate (reduces friction) and a football boot (increases friction)

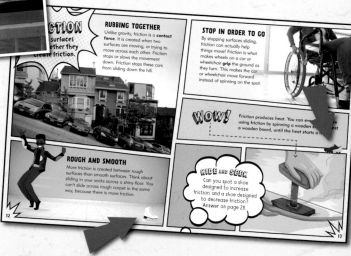

RUBBING TOGETHER
Unlike gravity, friction is a **contact force**. It is created when two surfaces are moving, or trying to move across each other. Friction stops or slows the movement down. Friction stops these cars from sliding down the hill.

STOP IN ORDER TO GO
By stopping surfaces sliding, friction can actually help things move! Friction is what makes wheels on a car or wheelchair **grip** the ground as they turn. This makes the car or wheelchair move forward instead of spinning on the spot.

WOW! Friction produces heat. You can even start a fire using friction by spinning a wooden stick against a wooden board, until the heat starts a fire.

ROUGH AND SMOOTH
More friction is created between rough surfaces than smooth surfaces. Think about sliding in your socks across a shiny floor. You can't slide across rough carpet in the same way, because there is more friction.

HIDE AND SEEK
Can you spot a shoe designed to increase friction, and a shoe designed to decrease friction? Answer on page 28.

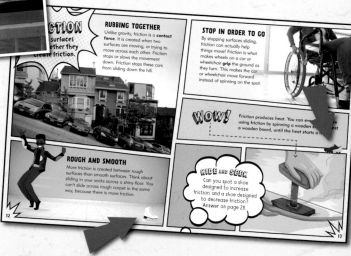

12

13

Page 15

Your turn By moving the grains of rice closer together, the wooden chopstick touches more of the grains of rice. This increases the overall friction between the rice and the chopstick, allowing the rice to grip the chopstick. When the chopstick is lifted, it stays stuck to the rice, and the whole bottle is lifted into the air.

Page 17

What am I? The lorry will experience more air resistance than the bicycle because it is larger, and it can go faster.

Page 19

What am I? I'm a pair of flippers.

Page 23

Hide and Seek A bar magnet

Page 25

What am I? I'm a **compass**.

GLOSSARY

air resistance a force that slows down objects that are moving through the air

applied to put into use

attract when an object pulls another object towards it

compass an object used to find out which direction north is

contact force a force that needs to actually touch an object to have an effect

friction a force that slows down or stops two surfaces from sliding against each other

gravity a pulling force, and the force that makes dropped objects fall to the floor

grip to stick to or hold on to a surface or an object

hard drive part of a computer where information is stored

liquid a material that is runny and doesn't hold a fixed shape

magnet an object that pulls certain metal objects towards it

magnetic field the area that a magnet can affect

magnetic force a pulling force, and the force that pulls on some types of metal

non-contact force a force that doesn't have to touch an object to have an effect on it

oars poles with a flat part at the end, used to row a boat

orbit when something constantly moves in a circle around something else

pole one of the two ends of a magnet

propel to drive or push something forwards

repel when an object pushes other objects away from it

streamlined when something is made into a pointy shape to reduce resistance

water resistance a force that slows down objects moving through water

INDEX